Yes, We Do Come with Directions

Instructions for a Happy Life

ROB CIMINELLI

PAGE PUBLISHING
Conneaut Lake, PA

First originally published by Page Publishing 2023

ISBN 979-8-88960-411-2 (pbk)
ISBN 979-8-88960-451-8 (hc)
ISBN 979-8-88960-428-0 (digital)

Printed in the United States of America

I dedicate this book to my handsome, loving ten-year-old grandson Ryder Andrew Ciminelli (love you, buddy); my beautiful eight-year-old granddaughter Aria Rose Shriver (love you, princess); my grandson Mark Leonard who is now three years old (love you, buddy); and lastly, our beautiful one-year-old granddaughter Isabel Leonard (love you, baby girl).

Contents

Foreword

Rob Ciminelli is an interesting, gifted, and unique person. He possesses an ability to truly listen to people and offer advice and direction in areas of their life that they are struggling in. Rob helps them to see their life with a new perspective! His effectiveness comes from his deep empathy and strong common sense, which leads nearly every time to that person improving and enjoying their life in a way that they had not been able to do before. What a gift he has to enable people to overcome their challenges and build a dream and a vision to lead a happy, fulfilling, and productive life.

- Scott Bieler, President & CEO
West Herr Automotive Group

Introduction

These are suggestions for you on how to read this book and get the most out of it to maximize the results you would love to see in your life.

- When I read self-development books, I like to start by reading the book all the way through once. Then I go back and start over with an even deeper dive. Whichever way you choose, I invite you to get a pen, a highlighter, and a notebook to take notes.
- This is not a race. Read this book at your own pace. The goal is to apply what you are learning as you read, but you can have fun while you are learning.
- Everyone reading this book is in a different place and at a different stage in life. Highlight, underline, and take notes on what resonates with you.
- If you apply what you learn in the coming pages, life will get easier for you.
- Read over and over—a chapter a day, a page a day, or just a couple of sentences.
- Give yourself the gift of creating and implementing your own daily practice. I share my daily practice in chapter 16, My Daily Practice.

What you will find on the following pages are life lessons that I have been learning all my life, but most importantly, a deeper study over the last twenty years. As the title says we do come with directions. The good news is, you do not have to reinvent the wheel. Everything we need to learn is right at our fingertips.

You may ask, "Rob, what inspired you to write this book?" Since I started my coaching practice, I have had the great pleasure of helping hundreds of people. The idea for this book became a way that I could touch thousands of more lives and possibly millions. Why not? You can be one of those people by reading and applying what you learn here in the pages that follow. I am inviting you right here and right now to decide that what you will learn here, you will apply. Your life can get much easier, happier, and you can be filled with greater joy. Would it be okay with you if your life got easier? *Yes*, great. :o)

Another reason I decided to write this book is that my inner voice has been calling me to do so. Have you ever been nudged to do something, and it would not leave you alone? My mentor, life coach, and friend Mary Morrissey calls it her inspired voice for truth.

Have you ever wondered and asked yourself, What have I done with my life? Will my being here have mattered? I can tell you that the answer is yes. You and I would not be here and breathing if we did not matter. So as I came to the realization that I do matter, the next question I asked myself was, Did I make an impact? As I was meditating on this, a thought came to me: Why don't I share what I teach in a book? I can touch many more lives, make a greater impact, and I could leave it as a legacy to my grandchildren Ryder, Aria, Mark, Isabel, and the grandchildren to follow.

I have seen clients' entire families change because of one family member learning and applying the principles I will be sharing here in the following pages.

I want to start off by thanking all the people that made this endeavor possible. Starting with my beautiful, loving, and supportive wife, Karen Ciminelli. I love you so much. Thank you, thank you, thank you.

The Great Family I was born into—. My Wonderful Mom and Dad, my sisters Gail and Jo, my brother Rich, and my twin brother Ron. Yes, we have a special bond. If I were given the opportunity to start all over again from birth, I feel blessed in saying that I would choose the same family.

My beautiful daughter Renee. What a joy you have brought to my heart over the years, the tough times that life threw at us when you were just a little girl. You were the reason and the fuel that kept me going. My bonus sons Steven and Eric, bonus daughter Deborah, and all my new family through Karen. Also, all my great friends over the years.

My Mentors/Teachers

Mary Morrissey—you are my life coach, mentor, and friend that helped me move this work from thought to form. If not for you, Mary, I would not be doing this work, touching so many lives and experiencing the happiness and freedom I now get to enjoy. Thank you so, so much!

Rhonda Byrne, for the documentary called *The Secret* that came out back in 2006. This set me on a much deeper study and my path. I have had the privilege of meeting and working with numerous teachers from *The Secret* panel including Mr. Bob Proctor.

Last but certainly not least, all the wonderful people that I have had the great honor and privilege to teach and serve. Many of you are now my dear friends. Thank you for trusting in me.

CHAPTER 1

The Story of How I Was Led to This Work

Back in 2005, I had a job for ten years that was just not bringing me life anymore. I was good at it and made a great living, but to be honest, I thought it was sucking the life out of me. Have you ever felt that way? A long-life friend of mine's sister convinced me to take an interview at a job that had "the grass is greener on the other side" look and feel. That was all it had, but I was grateful for her help. I will leave that right there. I had some savings and was confident enough that I would find something, so I resigned at the end of September 2006. Looking back now with what I have learned over the past fifteen years, I would have been even better at those jobs. I also know now for certain that those jobs were not my destiny.

As I was looking for opportunities, setting up interviews, the October Surprise ice storm hit Buffalo, New York. It was the night of October 13 and the morning of the fourteenth. The time was short; but the damage was devastating—trees, cable, phone, and power lines falling and electric transformers blowing up. It was kind of scary.

Tens of thousands of people lost power. We were out of power for almost two weeks. The temperature was in the forties. I put all the refrigerated items in coolers, filled them with ice, and buried them in the icy snow that nature had brought us. My daughter Renee and I threw on warmer clothes and extra blankets. Against all advice, I had the oven on with the door open, and I had big pots of water boiling to get heat through the house and use for cooking and washing.

Continuing with my job search, with my laptop and my camping lamp by my side, I set up appointments for interviews. I met a gentleman that, at first impression, was highly successful. He was dressed very well in a navy-blue suit; he was wearing a Rolex watch, and he pulled up in a new Hummer. His family owned a chain of businesses, but he informed me in our meeting that those businesses were not the cause of his success. He went on to tell me that his success was the result of his supplemental health drink business and that I could be part of it, and he would help me. He invited me to a rollout he was doing at a large mall in our area. I was introduced to the business, the product, and some of his associates, including his mom. We then proceeded to go out to a kiosk and tables set up in the middle of what was a busy area. We were asked to talk to people about the product and have them try it. We also were to try and sell it to them and ask for their phone numbers and email addresses.

His mom was running the show pretty much. We really hit it off great. We generated great conversations with the shoppers in the mall. We enjoyed a fun, successful evening meeting people and having them see and taste the product. We took down many phone numbers and emails. As a result of our great efforts, the gentlemen gave me a basket of development teaching books and DVDs from many of the greats, such as Napoleon Hill, Louise Hay, Dr. Wayne Dyer, Zig Ziglar, and many others. As I mentioned in my introduction, I had always been attracted to and loved reading and listening to self-development material.

The big one for me in the basket was *The Secret* DVD by Rhonda Byrne, the original. It had just been released, but I had not heard about it. As I watched in the dark on my computer in a cold house with my camping lamp, I had never felt more alive. *The Secret* was about the Law of Attraction and how to apply it. I had always done well in my life, but I had never heard of this universal law. Even as I was experiencing a defining moment for me. I had another side of me wondering, How can this be? And how am I forty-six years old and had never heard of this? I watched it daily and told everyone about it. I bought copies and gave them to people. Thinking back now, some of the people including my family may have thought I was crazy. Later, as I met Mary Morrissey, my mentor/life coach, I told her the story, and she told me she did the same thing earlier when she learned of the Law of Attraction. She called it her beating of the drum days. I did rein it in a bit, but I have never lost the fire that was stirred up in me on that day. I decided I would purchase all the material I could from all the great teachers that were in *The Secret* DVD. I also found others such as Louise Hay and Dr. Wayne Dyer (my wife's favorite).

As I continued to study and apply what I was learning, I became very aware that we are the masters of our destiny, if we decide that we will be. This great life energy was coming over me, and it continued to increase my hunger for more. As previously noted, I had always done well, but now knowing with certainty that I, we, could do even better. The people around me hadn't heard of the Law of Attraction. If they had, they were not applying it. Or they tried and came to the belief that it did not work for them. I decided then that I would get it to work for me. After all, it is a law, right?

I decided not to take on the supplemental health drink membership, for it just didn't feel like a match at the time. I then sat down and wrote out that I would receive multiple interview opportunities and offers in the next couple of weeks. One job was a great company that my eldest sister, Gail, and her soon-to-be husband Rick had worked at for almost thirty years. Another one was an insurance company, and the last opportunity was a bank. I chose where my sister worked. I focused on it, visualized, and with their support, believed I would get the job. Well, I did, starting as what was called an agency temp and was set to start in December-January timeframe. I was trained during the day and would soon go up to second shift. I went back to my pen and paper and wrote that I would be promoted to full-time company employee within one year.

It was made clear to me that being promoted to full-time company employee would not happen. Over the next couple of months, I met numerous agency temp people that were there for years. One nice gentleman was on his eighth year. I worked extremely hard, put in overtime, and learned other skills in neighboring departments; and I held firm in my belief. I was promoted in eleven months. Happy dance for me.

My other dreams were money for a new roof, a new sports car, give to charities, remodel my home, and enjoy time with my daughter Renee. I did just that, and life was getting easier, and I was much happier.

I was working second shift, and my new desire was to be on first shift. Again, I was told that will never happen. People had been there forever and had not been able to do that. At first, that did not make sense to me, and I knew in my gut that was not the answer. Applying the Law of Attraction, being grateful for where I was while calling in my desire, I was moved to first shift in—yes, you guessed it—eleven months.

One evening, I was really connecting to the truth that this really, really worked. *What If I could bring in my new love, my life partner?* You see, I had divorced many years ago when Renee was four years old, and I became a single dad. I had tried dating over the years and had the blessings of wonderful people that came into my life. For some reason, be it my decision or theirs, the relationships just did not work out. You begin to wonder, What was wrong with me? What was I doing? Looking back now, I simply just needed more growth. It really was me. But now, I am ready. I can feel it in my bones. So what was a guy to do? Do what he had been learning: write down exactly what he would love.

I did exactly that; I wrote out everything I liked and wanted in a woman—characteristics such as honest, loving, hardworking, family-oriented, intelligent, caring, supportive, and fun; things we would do together and how we would get along. I wrote down some physical aspects such as a great smile, and she would have green or blue eyes. Karen has both. Not one green eye and one blue eye, they just changed colors. I also was aware that I was attracted to woman that had curves over, say, somebody very thin. I had one person I shared this with say that was kind of shallow. Not at all. We want to be attracted to our partner, right? I wrote out my vision of my partner the week of Halloween 2008, and I met my love, Karen, on December 6, 2008. Yes, approximately thirty-six days later. :o)

Maybe you have a desire in your heart to have your life partner. You can if you decide. I have helped many people call this part of their dream into their lives. Life continued to move along wonderfully. We are as happy now and even happier from the day we met. We dated for almost two years, and then we were married in August of 2010.

With the Law of Attraction still running strong in my life, I decided to take an even deeper dive and study more of the great life transformative teachers of our time. I learned that you could hire these people to be your mentor, your life coach. I was super impressed with Bob Proctor and Jack Canfield in *The Secret*. I called their offices and had complimentary strategy sessions with their associates to see if I could work with them. I loved the calls, but I had never invested in myself in that way.

I learned right in that moment what a money paradigm was. When I was on the call with Bob Proctor's associate, he asked me to have my wife join in on the call. He made me an offer, and looking back now, it wasn't that much money, but I was really thrown back. We were asked to take forty-eight hours, think it over, and then call him. We hung up, and Karen said, "I have never heard you be so nervous. Are you okay?" Jack Canfield's program was the same investment. Looking back now, it really was not about the money. Did I have it, or could I come up with the money? Yes. It was because I had never invested in myself in that way before. It was my paradigm. Whenever we move into unchartered territory or something new, we may feel some rattle or discomfort, but that doesn't mean it isn't the right choice for us.

As I thought about their offers, an affiliate email came in from Bob Proctor about Mary Morrissey. I got to watch some posts of hers, signed up for a free webinar, and I just knew she was going to be my mentor. I loved how she delivered this great knowledge and that she was like a mother figure. Mary also had an amazing spiritual presence about her, so I decided that, without a doubt, she was the one to be my life coach, the person I would begin this journey with. I shared with Karen that she was the one to mentor me. The paradigm was breaking down not only because the investment was a bit lower but because I could now see the value of what I was being offered. Karen and I went to dinner at our favorite restaurant and had a great conversation. Karen, without hesitation, said, "Go for it. You work hard, and you know what you want. Invest in yourself, and I believe you will love this, and I think this will be good for you."

The first course I took with Mary was three months long, and it changed my life exponentially for the better.

It was like all I was learning times a hundred. Remember I said earlier that I not only didn't know about these laws and how they worked but neither did the people around me. I went to a live seminar Mary was holding in California. I found out there that I could go to her coaching institute to learn how to teach this work, while having Mary and her team support me while I was learning. I decided to move forward and make the investment required. The following training was five times the initial investment, but even so, that was a much easier investment for me. My goal now was to become a life mastery consultant and teach this great work to others.

The voice of doubt, which I have learned how to speak to and now teach others, said to me, "How are you going to do that? You work fifty-five- and sixty-five-hour work weeks." Again, I received Karen's heartfelt and supportive blessing, and I was off and running. I earned my certification at the Life Mastery Institute in Los Angeles. I then opened my practice Dreams to Manifestation, LLC, in August of 2012.

I started teaching at night and whenever I could the next couple of years while staying immersed in Mary's teachings. I have had the privilege of having Bob Proctor mentor me as well. I had the honor of working at that job with my sister that I mentioned. It was a great place to work if you want to work for someone else. I chose to leave there and gave my notice in September of 2014. I then received the prestigious life coach award of excellence in California five days later. This will forever be one of the special moments in my life. A great little story about that.

I was done with my live training, and I was going to meet some friends at the beach. Mary's daughter Jennifer came up to me and asked me if I could hold off and go put my suit back on, for Mary would like me to say a few words. It was to over three hundred people that were eager to learn more about what I was learning. At first, I thought, *Oh boy*, but I knew I would be okay. That was when Mary gave me this great introduction and then called me up on the stage. When I was done, I received a standing ovation. Then Mary shared some great words about me and handed me the award of excellence for life coaching. :o)

I am so grateful for all my life experiences, all the people I have had the pleasure of teaching, and now getting that same pleasure of teaching you, my new friend, reading these pages. My passion and vision are that this is not a book you read, feel entertained or inspired for a moment, and then you place it back on the shelf. My desire is that you decide to make it a part of you and your daily life. I cannot write you a guarantee, but I will tell you what Mary always says to me, "This works if you work it."

C H A P T E R 2

Desire

Like me, you have most likely picked up this book for you are wanting more, looking to grow or expand your life in some way. The word *desire* has a sacredness to it. *Desire* comes from the Latin word meaning "of the sire"_or "of the Father."_When I first heard that, I took it to mean that whatever you call your higher power (God, spirit, source, or universe), that power is at work in you and wants what you want too. That means it will support and guide you to your dreams, if you know what they are. What I have found as I meet people is that they don't have dreams, are not clear on what they want, have given up on their dreams, and/or came to the belief that they could not or would not achieve them.

The universe loves specificity. We want to get very, very clear on the lives we would love living. What I learned over time was there is something bigger than me and my physical presence. Again, you can call it what you like—God, source, energy, universe, or infinite intelligence. Without touching or hurting yourself, you cannot stop yourself

10

from breathing or stop your heart from beating even one time. Why? Because you, we are not doing it.

The desires of our hearts speak to us if we will listen. We have a mental faculty called intuition, that inner knowing knows the things that will bring us joy and the things that will not bring us joy. We want to become more familiar with that inner voice of guidance and make friends with it. Think of it like a muscle. The more you work it, the more it grows.

You see, we are moved by our longing and our discontent. Our longings and discontent will direct you to where you want to go. Let us begin with our longings. Longings are clear and usually will not leave us alone. That intuitive part of you is innate in knowing what we would love. Have you ever heard that voice speak to you, probably more than once and sometimes the same topic over and over? I know I have and still do at times; although I am a good student of that voice now. It says, "Do this, do that, go here, go there, turn here, do it, for you would be great at this."

I had a client do just that. Ever since she was nine years of age, she wanted to be a nurse. It called her throughout her life. When she became my client, she was forty-two years old and had already raised a beautiful family. She said to me, "What do I do now?" My answer was always, "What would you love?" Her answer came very quickly, "I always wanted to be a nurse. I have known that since I was nine years old. My mother told me I was too stupid to do that. 'Who do you think you are?'"

"You know now that is not true." So I said, "There you have it. Go do that. It has been calling you that long."

Her response was "I can't do that now. I am forty-two years old."

My answer was, "Who says?"

She now has her nursing degree, is a nurse, and is studying to be a physician's assistant. She is just beaming with purpose and joy. Now I ask you, What has been calling you? Take a minute and give this some thought.

Now, let us talk about discontent. Discontent can also come from that all-knowing part of us. This part of us is letting us know that something is not a match or something we are doing or experiencing is not bringing us life. In a nutshell, it is something we don't like, and we just want it to go away, just disappear.

For example: Your body is aching or hurting. A relationship is not going the way you would like, for you want more love, more fun, a deeper connection. Your business or career is not going the way you would like. You want more time or money or both. You would like to have your own home or have a different home. Whatever it is for you, the discontent is not there to make us feel bad. Discontent is there to say "Not this way. There's a better way." Discontent is not bad news. Discontent is there to serve us. It drives us to want more and will fuel us to make a change. If we ignore the call, the thing we are discontent about may get worse.

Why? Remember the Law of Attraction is at work. What we focus on and think about on a regular basis, we get more of. You see it works its way, not ours. When my mentor Mary hears me fighting for my limitations and is trying to help me shift, she will say, "Have it your way." I would be like, *no!* I do not want to do it my way. My way was not working, so I wanted to learn how it works. It is funny; we will hire someone to help and support us, and then we don't apply what they know works.

This reminds me of a conversation that I had with a longtime dear friend. He was complaining about his health, relationship issues, and tough times and money issues. I had noticed a trend that often when we talked, we would be having the same conversation. He knows the work I do, and being good friends, I said, "You know you are going to get more things to complain about." He went on to tell me that he prays every night that it would change.

I let him know that this great God/universal presence designed it to work this way. It is okay to pray for help or what others might say, hold an intention for what you want. But if you do not change, starting with your thoughts, words, and then actions, things will not change. The good news here for all of us is, we can change it. My friend said, "Then what do I do?" I helped him figure out what he would love, and we talked about the things that were keeping him stuck, starting with his thoughts and words. I asked him to do a grateful exercise three times a day. Each of the three times, he should name ten things he is grateful for and really feel them. Being grateful will move you into a higher frequency. When feeling yourself worried about money, just say, "I am grateful that all my obligations are being met" or "Money flows to me freely and easily from multiple sources on a regular continual basis."

You see, many of us are wanting and even expecting change, and we are not doing anything different while waiting for the change to come in. You may have heard the new definition of insanity, "repeating the same thing over and over again and expecting a different result."

I have studied many great people, past and present, and they may not agree on everything, but the thing I found in common was they believe our subconscious mind is connected to the source that breathes us. It never sleeps. Intuition is connected to that energy that knows all, and we can tap into that source energy if we choose.

The title of this book is *Yes, We Do Come with Directions*. The word *direction* is defined as "the path that something or someone takes, the path that must be taken to reach a specific place, the way in which something is starting to develop or the way you are facing."

Which way are you facing? Are you facing in the direction you want to go? You see, we are creating our lives by design or default. If you do not have a design for your life, a blueprint, a map, or a vision of where you want to go, you are creating by default. I didn't like hearing that the first time I heard it because I was creating by default. The good news is, if you are creating your life by design, with a clear vision, you will move into that direction. More good news for you is, we will be covering how to create and write your vision in a coming chapter.

But first, why a vision? Everything is created twice, first in thought and then in form. Look at your surroundings right now. This book your reading is a thought. The room you are sitting in reading this book was also a thought. The clothes you are wearing, the car you drive, the paper I wrote this on when I started, and the computer I am typing this into right now, they were all a thought before they became a thing. It was so empowering when I heard this. That meant I truly was a cocreator. You are too.

You see with the Law of Attraction, everything you focus on expands. What you think of throughout your day is what you will attract. A clear vision of the life you love makes life easier. Having a vision brings us to our yeses and our nos very easily and quickly. If you are clear on what you want, you know what matches, and you also know what does not match. For example, "No, thank you, this does not match my vision for the person I want to be in the world," "This does not match the dreams I have for me, my health, my business, my family," or "Yes, this is an exact match."

As I help my clients create a vision, they will say, "This feels wonderful, but I don't believe or don't know how I will bring it into reality." Let us speak to the belief first. Some clients share with me things like, "I will believe it when I see it." It is the just the opposite. You will see it when you believe it. If you hold it in your mind, you can hold it in your hand. The people that you consider having great success, the kind of success you would like to experience in your life, have a vision. And they believe they will obtain it. It has been said that only 10 percent of us have a vision. When I was at an event with Bob Proctor, now called the *Grandfather of Transformation*, he said he believes it is now one in a hundred moving to one in a thousand of us, after studying and teaching this work for sixty-one years. I am choosing to be the one out of the one hundred or one thousand that Bob was talking about. You can be as well if you choose.

Now, let us address if you are having thoughts like "I have a dream, but I don't know how to get there." *More good news!* You don't have to know how; you have to know *what*. When I first heard this, I thought I was hearing things, or they are out of their minds. How can I do, be, or have something I want without knowing how to get it? What is funny is that inner knowing, my intuition, heard some truth in it. I have found it to be true, and so have my clients. Your vision is the key. Once you are clear on the what, the how will be shown to you.

Dr. Martin Luther King said, "Take the first step in faith. You don't have to see the whole staircase, just take the first step."

Albert Einstein said, "Everything is energy, and that's all there is to it. Match the frequency of the reality you want, and you cannot help but get that reality. It can be no other way. This is not philosophy. This is physics."

The reality you want is the dream life you describe living in your vision. Match your frequency, your thoughts, and your words. Act as if you are living the life you love. Be grateful right now as if it were so. How would you feel if you were living the life you love? Feel that now.

If you have attended one of my webinars or workshops or have worked with me, you will hear me speak on frequency. I also ask my clients often, "What seeds are you planting?" You will want to ask yourself this question throughout your day. I always ask, "If you plant corn, what do you get?" The audience goes silent as if I were asking a trick question. I repeat the question until somebody answers corn. Yes. Do you want to receive a great harvest of what you have been planting, yesterday, last week, last month, last year? If your answer is yes, keep planting and watering those seeds. If your answer is no, you can choose to plant new seeds. This is the Law of Attraction at work.

CHAPTER 3

The Law of Attraction and Your Vibration

There are laws and principles that govern this universe. The Law of Attraction is one of these laws. As I mentioned earlier, people we consider great or have done what we call great things applied this law, some unconsciously, but nonetheless, they were applying them. Not everyone applying the law are consciously aware that they are, and nonetheless, the laws work in their favor. Oprah Winfrey is a great example. She was also really taken by *The Secret* when it came out. She had many of *The Secret* panel on her show. Oprah said on that show that she didn't know the name or that it had a name, but in fact, she had been doing this since she was young.

The Law of Attraction is called a law because it is always working. Think for one moment of the law of gravity. If you step off the roof of your house, you are going to hit the ground. No maybes about it. Now, let us think about the law of electricity. We do not have to know how electricity works. If you go to turn a lamp on, and it doesn't come on, you wouldn't say that the law of electricity doesn't work for you. You would think, maybe the bulb burned out or maybe the lamp is unplugged. If both of those are good, you would then check the breakers. If still not working, you would call an electrician.

As I meet people at my events or people that are referred to me, I will have a conversation with them about what is going on in their lives, what challenges they are facing, and where they are going. When I ask the "where are they going" question, it lets me know if they have a vision for their lives, dreams and goals of where they want to be three, five, ten years from now. I then let them know that people thinking about their dreams, writing them down are connecting themselves to the Law of Attraction. Employers still ask potential candidates on interviews, Where do you see yourself in three to five years? Why? They want to hire somebody with purpose, vision, and goals.

I then say to them when you are clear on the life you would love to live, the universe through the Law of Attraction will bring you the opportunities needed to support your dreams. You will get a phone call, meet somebody, or receive an email out of the blue. By the way, there is no "out of the blue." There are no coincidences. When I first heard that, I was like, "Really?" The answer I was given is the same as I will give you. Yes, really, absolutely.

The reply I get often is, "I have heard of the Law of Attraction. I have even tried to apply it, but it doesn't work for me." Being a law, this cannot be true. The law of gravity is not just for the few. The Law of Attraction will work if you work it its way. Remember, what we focus on expands.

If we are feeling like something is not working for us, then we are giving more attention to what we are not liking and not wanting in our lives.

We all have things in our lives we want to be expanding in. While we are calling those things in, we want to make it a practice of being grateful for what we can be grateful for. Michael Beckwith said, "Being grateful opens the door for more good to come to you." Another one of our greatest teachers, Louise Hay, said, "The more grateful you are, the more you get to be grateful for." Being grateful puts you on the frequency of receiving. I have my clients start right there.

Every morning think about ten things you are grateful for. Feel the feelings around your being grateful for those things. I am not suggesting this is all you do, but if it is all you did do, your life would expand exponentially.

Let us now talk about our frequency. The frequency we are in is what creates the vibration. The vibration is then sent out to the universe, and the Law of Attraction is activated. What starts off this chain of events is our thoughts. What you predominately think about, whether it be considered good or bad, creates a feeling. That feeling becomes the vibration you are in, and that is what you are sending out.

As I mentioned earlier, if you plant corn, you get corn. It is as if you are a magnet. What you send out is what comes back to you. Think of it like the TV in your living room or a radio. The TV and the radio are receiving multiple stations. Some people have five hundred channels to choose from. You would not just sit there and watch or listen to something you didn't like. I wish I didn't have to watch or listen to this. *No*, you would change the channel, the frequency, to something you would like. We want to be doing that with our thoughts.

CHAPTER 4

Condition-Based Thinking and Paradigms

Paradigm is a word that has been talked about quite a bit over the last ten to fifteen years, and we are hearing it more and more often. Someone may say in a training or a seminar that we must change our paradigm or switch our paradigm. When I first heard the word, I was like, "What is that? And how can I change something I never heard of?"

A paradigm is just a thought about a thing or a topic that we have come to believe over time—a habitual way of thinking, believing, or even acting if you will. This doesn't mean it is either good or bad for you, for it can be both. What I have found early on in myself and in the work with my clients, is that we have paradigms we don't even know are there. We are just not aware of them.

What we are talking about is being awakened to what we have learned and determining whether it is serving us, our dreams, our families, and even our being, our health. Again, paradigms can serve us. Some examples are as follows: (1) I can do this job in my sleep, (2) I can do this with my eyes closed, or (3) I know I drove here, but I don't remember anything about the drive. It is really because you didn't. Your paradigm/subconscious pattern took over and drove you there. You were on what we sometimes call autopilot.

Extensive research is now showing that from the time we wake up, our subconscious is running us, 95 percent of our day. Again, some of this is great, but it means we are consciously running our minds only 5 percent of our day. Through work like this and continuous study and application, we will create a heightened awareness and be what Buddha called being awake.

You see what happens is, we have been trained to be reactive, though not intentionally. The training that we come up in is said to come down for at least five generations. I believe it is much longer. We call it conditioned-based thinking. This doesn't make our parents, aunts, uncles, brothers, sisters, teachers, neighbors, coaches, or even the media bad or wrong. They were just doing the best they could with what they were taught. For some of you, this may not seem true, for you were brought up by people that didn't have your best interest at heart and may have even been abusive. For that, I am deeply sorry. The good news is, you will not have to carry that around with you any longer. You can choose to respond and not react. Reaction is knee jerk, what you have learned and have always done. Your go-to. Responding how you want to is a learned skill, and you can learn it quickly. You stop, take breaths, and count to three. You then can choose to respond in a way that you want to. I will be covering that in a later chapter on forgiveness.

Let us now cover some conditioned-based thinking statements you may have heard over time. You may have thought at one time that these don't even make sense. Let us have some fun with these. I am going to extend the last word out of the phrase to the end of the sentence. See if you know them.

1. You have to know somebody to get … ahead.
2. It takes money to make … money.
3. Better safe than … sorry.
4. You can't teach an old dog new …tricks.
5. Curiosity killed the … cat.
6. Don't bite off more than you can … chew.
7. Nice guys finish … last.
8. You can't have your cake and eat it … too.
9. Money is the root of all … evil.
10. It's too good to be … true.
11. Money doesn't grow on … trees.

How did you know all the answers to these? Did you grow up on my street? LOL! These phrases and many more have been used throughout our lives. You might be inclined to say, "Well, Rob, they are just sayings. We're kidding around most of the time when we think or say them." Remember, it doesn't matter.

Your thoughts are creative, and if you say and hear something enough times, your subconscious will make it true for you, even a lie. You can watch somebody you know repeat something you know is not true, but they have told the story so many times it has become true for them. It becomes a hidden belief or a paradigm. A belief that we have entertained repeatedly until we make it true in our lives. The scary part is, we don't even know we are doing it. Well, not anymore. My passion for writing this book was for you to gain the awareness that you or others around you are doing this, and you can say, "No more."

I would like to share one of the phrases that I heard quite often growing up. I was brought up in the '60s and '70s, and the phrase "money doesn't grow on trees" was said to me often. As I mentioned earlier, I was blessed with great, loving parents. I wouldn't trade that experience, but they would say that often. Why? Because they didn't have the money I was asking for, and that's what they heard growing up, so they said it to me.

You might be thinking, *Well, Rob, money doesn't grow on trees.* Yes, you are correct, and I know that is physically true. The saying "money doesn't grow on trees" is a paradigm, a subconscious habitual belief that money is hard. What do you suppose a person growing up hearing these types of statements believes? Money is hard. I cannot have things I want because I cannot afford them. This will get imbedded into your subconscious without your knowing it, and it will be difficult for you to afford things. You will remind yourself, and even your children and your grandchildren, that money doesn't grow on trees.

This is a story I would like to share with you about my dad and me in a car ride. This was way back in the year 1972–1973. It was a school year, and I was looking at some of the extracurricular activities being offered at my school. I grew an interest or a liking to what was called the audio-visual club. This club would record things on this close-circuit television recording unit with cameras. These were big machines. We can do that all on our cell phones now. We would set up for auditorium movies or set up class projectors for movies in class for the teachers as well as set up and tear down lights and the sound equipment for the school band or the basketball and football games. We would even get to travel with them when they played outside of the school.

I decided I wanted in. I was given some paperwork to read and have parents sign, and I would receive an AV badge. For this to be finalized, I needed ten dollars. Now mind you, my dad was the greatest example of a human being I have ever witnessed in my life, still to this day, and he left this physical plane over twenty years ago. So I got up the nerve while we were on this car ride to ask him for the ten dollars. He never was one to shout or get angry, and he didn't then either.

But he said, "Where am I going to get an extra ten dollars so quickly? What are we, the Rockefellers?" Now, I knew who the Rockefellers were—everyone did—one of the richest families in the country. I never forgot that. I offered to do extra chores or whatever I could. I told him I would shovel more driveways and sidewalks, cut people's lawns, and that I would wash more cars, which I loved doing, to pay him back. "You see, Dad, I need this by Friday, for they only have so many people allowed to sign up to be in the AV club." Not sure what he did, but he and my mom came up with the money. I met my end of the bargain to pay him back, but he wouldn't take it.

My final point to this story is my dad was a great person, a great man, a genius if you will. He could do anything. He built homes, and he could fix anything—watches, cars, TVs, washing machines. It did not matter what it was. He was just a genuinely good person. He loved everyone and would help anyone any time of day or night, like I shared earlier. He embodied in his heart and soul to love unconditionally and acted as if we were all one. He worked two and three jobs his whole life so my mom could stay at home and raise us.

I look back now, and I can see it was not easy for him, but he never complained and did it with joy. After all I have learned thus far, I realize his life would have been easier, but he had paradigms that were blocking him in the financial arena. There just had to be. Because from the outside looking in, he deserved so much more. In the end, we may not have had all the finer things in life, but you wouldn't have known it. We had great love and support. We were rich in that way for sure.

One thing I know ran in me and hundreds of my clients is the phrase "I cannot afford that." They tell their kids, "Put that down. We cannot afford that." Looking at your bank balance, it may be true. My invitation to you is to change "I cannot, we cannot afford that" to "This is not a priority right now." You see, we tell ourselves, our kids, and others we cannot afford things on a regular basis. Your subconscious takes this on as truth and, worse yet, helps you to not afford things. Remember, whatever you tell your subconscious enough, it will take over automatically. It will be a challenge for a person hearing that they cannot afford things their whole life to then be able to afford things without breaking that paradigm or pattern of belief.

The things that are blocking you, me, and my dad were just simply beliefs we took on as truth—paradigms and condition-based thinking, habitual patterns of belief.

CHAPTER 5

More on Paradigms

I think it is important to talk about the thoughts and beliefs we have entertained and taken on as truth. I invite you to open your mind to the idea that it is possible that some of the things we have learned may not be true and do not serve you. You can bring up any topic in a full room of people, and you will receive different perspectives, even from siblings growing up in the same home at the same time. It is just their take on it and their understanding, their perception.

Where does that come from? It started the day we were born. From birth to the age of five years old, some six and seven years old, in that short timeframe, we have taken into our minds millions upon millions of bits of information. This information comes mainly from our parents, relatives, and caregivers at first and then from multiple sources— school, church, TV, radio, sports, neighbors, coaches, and activities we are involved in, even our young friends. Again, this doesn't make these people wrong. There is no judgment; it just is.

When I first learned this, I asked myself, Why would I, or anybody for that matter, allow this? We were just toddlers. We didn't know any better, and the people caring for us are all-knowing in our eyes. For the most part, they were, and they served us in the best way that they could. Another way that I answer this is, we do not have a conscious filter telling us something isn't true about us or something is wrong, and we are totally trusting. Even if we had a feeling that didn't sound right or feel right, we didn't know how to describe that feeling or express it.

You are probably thinking right now, Well, how do I change this? We do it with our conscious mind. Your conscious, awake mind is in control of your body/subconscious mind. You get to direct how you will operate it. I have helped hundreds of people do this. I have learned over time that a person makes this change for growth in one of two ways.

Option 1: A conscious decision to make change. Deliberate action to study, create, and apply the information being studied, like you are doing here. When you make this decision, questions will arise. How can I do this better? Who do I know that I can talk to? Who is living the kind of life I want to live? How can I do better with my health and my relationships? It starts with discipline and commitment. But the first and most important thing we can do is start working with our thoughts, noticing the thoughts we are having; and if they are not what we would love to experience, we remove and replace those thoughts with new thoughts that we would love.

Option 2: Sudden impact—this is when someone loses a job, is asked for a divorce, or gets into a serious accident or a serious health diagnosis like cancer or a loved one passes. You may have experienced this. If not, you probably know someone that has, and they decided to work on personal growth and changed their lives very quickly. The sudden impact brought them to consciousness, which then brings them to thoughts of making, moving toward the change they need.

CHAPTER 6

Conscious vs. Subconscious

Your subconscious never sleeps, and it has no sense of humor. It doesn't know or care what is right or wrong, true or untrue. It just believes what we tell it, even a lie. Have you ever had a dream and your body took it on as if it were real? You woke up and told someone that was so real. Your subconscious made it so. Overtime as we train our subconscious on whatever we choose, it will take over and do the work for you, with little or no help. This is a good thing if we are awake to how we are directing it.

Is it easy to start directing your mind to your choosing? No, if you have never done it or didn't know that you could. I assure you it will get easier because the subconscious mind will take it over for you. I want to share a great story that I heard from Napoleon Hill. Napoleon Hill was one of our greatest teachers. Back in the early 1900s, he was invited to Andrew Carnegie's home. Andrew Carnegie was the richest man in the world at the time. He wanted to find someone that would go and interview five hundred of the most successful people he knew and put the principles that he learned in a book.

He told him it would take him twenty years to do the research, and he would not be paid. Napoleon was a struggling young magazine writer at the time. His first thoughts were "Why on earth would he be asking me? Of all the people he knows, how could I be the one? He must not be as sharp as I thought he was after all." After about twenty seconds, something came over Napoleon, and he yelled out, "Yes, I will do it!"

It was a good thing, for it has been said that Andrew Carnegie was holding a stopwatch under his desk and had it timed to one minute. If Napoleon didn't answer within the minute, the opportunity would be lost. The book is called *Think and Grow Rich*. It did indeed take Napoleon Hill twenty years to gather the information and another five years to write the book. The book has been considered by many the greatest success book ever written.

Andrew Carnegie also taught and shared what he called the Choice with Napoleon Hill, and Napoleon went on to teach it as well. I will share it with you here and now. I invite you to open your heart and minds to the golden nuggets that were and are still being expressed here.

The Choice

> Everyone comes to the earth plane blessed
> with the privilege of controlling his mind
> and directing it toward whatever ends he
> may choose. But everyone brings over
> with him at birth the equivalent of two

sealed envelopes, one of which is clearly labeled:

"The Riches you may enjoy if you take possession of your own mind and direct it to the ends of your own choice."

And the other is labeled:

"The Penalties you must pay if you neglect to take possession of your mind and direct it." (Andrew Carnegie)

The Envelopes

Envelope 1: Riches

The riches you may enjoy if you take possession of your own mind and direct it to the ends of your own choice:

1. Sound health
2. Peace of mind
3. A labor of love of your own choice
4. Freedom from fear and worry
5. A positive mental attitude
6. Material riches of your own choice and quantity

Envelope 2: Penalties

The prices one must pay for neglecting to take possession of one's own mind:

1. Ill health

2. Fear and worry
3. Indecision and doubt
4. Frustration and discouragement throughout life
5. Poverty and want
6. A whole flock of evils consisting of envy, greed, jealousy, anger, hatred, and superstition

So which envelope do you choose? I teach this in my workshops and webinars. When I ask this question, the answer has always been envelope 1 every single time. The next question I have for you is, Will you do the work? Will you take possession of your mind and direct it? I am holding that your answer is a resounding yes here as well. If so, you can and you will, and I congratulate you. Take a moment and celebrate this life-changing decision you have just made.

Would you like to know more on how powerful your thinking is? The poem I share with you below is author unknown. I call it one of my greatest finds. I believe my first introduction was from my coach Mary. I read this regularly, and I share with my clients as well.

> I am your constant companion.
> I am your greatest helper or your heaviest
>   burden.
> I will push you onward or drag you down
>   to failure.
> I am completely at your command.
> Half the things you do, you might just as
>   well turn them over to me, and I will

be able to do them quickly and cor-
rectly if you just give me guidance.
I am easily managed, but you must be
firm with me.
Show me exactly what you want done,
what you want created, and I will
work on it automatically.
I am the servant of all great men and
woman, but, alas, I am also that
which brings failure to them as well.
Those who are great, I have made great.
Those who are failures, I have made
failures.
I am not a machine, but I work with the
precision of a fine machine, plus the
intelligence of the smartest person
you know.
You may run me for profit or run me for
ruin. It makes no difference to me.
Take me, train me, be firm with me, and I
will place the world at your feet.
Be easy with me, casual with me, con-
venient with me, and I will destroy
every dream you have.
WHO AM I? I am your *THINKING.*
("Who Am I," author unknown)

As I mentioned before you read this great poem, I
revisit this regularly. Why, you might ask. This poem
describes exactly how your mind works when you neglect

it. And how your mind will work if you take control of it and direct it. What I love about my work and the works of all the greats and people that are achieving great things is they know this, and they apply it. We are not going to do it perfectly, but we can become very good at it. I have had the pleasure of seeing thousands of people make great changes in their lives very quickly.

CHAPTER 7

Faith

As I was writing, I found it especially important to cover faith and how it applies to the work we are doing here. Let us start with the dictionary's definition of *faith*: "complete trust or confidence in someone or something."

This universe is governed by laws and principles. Some would say invisible laws. When we learn how to apply the laws and principles I am sharing in this book, we will be applying a great deal of what I like to call applied faith.

There was a time and place in my life when I would experience worry and doubt. Some people have added to worry and doubt, a great deal of anxiety. In my work and in my life, I have had many people tell me they have a strong faith. I tell them what I have learned. Worry and doubt are opposites of faith. If we had a strong faith, we would not be worrying, doubting, and experiencing anxiety to the extent that some people are. Talk about getting hit between the eyes, I was really thrown back by that, and maybe you just were as well.

Some link faith to their religion. They say "I have a strong belief in my God, my higher power," yet they are worrying and fretting. This is not faith. It is the opposite. You see, the truth is we are not practicing a strong faith if there is no clear evidence of it in our lives. A person with a strong faith is not full of anxiety and worry. They know that all is being worked out for their good and that all will be well. Even in the middle of what looks to be a major problem, we can have faith.

I remember as I was learning this and trying to apply it, I would think or say to myself, "Well, everybody worries." I have since found out that that is not true. We have been taught that, and yes, most people do, but not everyone. Worrying is considered normal, but it is not natural. Worrying is a learned behavior, and we can unlearn it. A person applying faith would answer a challenge in this way. This is what it looks like while it is getting solved. This is what it looks like while it's happening. What if it all worked out? How would I feel?

This includes when we are holding our visions and dreams, and we are taking the action we are being led to take, but nothing appears to be happening. Faith would say, "This is what it looks like while it is happening." The next statement was another game changer for me, and I use it often: "The absence of evidence is not evidence of absence." You are not different than people that think in this way. They just learned how. You have everything within you to learn how to apply this. I have seen countless people become great at this.

Faith applied to feeling overwhelmed. What is happening with us when we are feeling overwhelmed? When we are feeling overwhelmed, we are making the thing we are overwhelmed about bigger than we are. That then creates fear, uncertainty, and doubt. If we are feeling these feelings and emotions, we are going to be overwhelmed. The life skill I invite you to apply here is this: nothing you are experiencing is bigger than you and what is breathing you. Once I got this, everything changed for me and my clients, and life got a whole lot easier. This is faith applied.

Another great tool when going through what appears to be a challenge, a tough circumstance or event: make it only part of you. We make it all of us. An event happens. It ruined my day, it ruined everything, and it ruined my life. Unless a very tragic situation, this is not usually the case. We have learned to make it all of us, and we don't have to. It is just another way that we have learned to be, and we don't have to. We get to choose.

If you are experiencing a tough trial in some aspect of your life, move from worry, fear, and anxiety and ask solution-based questions. What if it all worked out? What does that look like? Picture that it is all working out. What if you woke up tomorrow and it was all resolved? Feel that feeling now. Do what you can. If nothing comes to mind, just be open that an idea, and a solution is on the way. Trust that it is all getting resolved.

I have been asked often about life events around that are seen to be negative and not good, even scary. I start with breathing. I take multiple breaths. I remind myself that worry and panic never ever helps. These emotions are not productive and do not lead us to feeling better. We can be concerned or have some fear, but we do not have to let the fear have us. We do not deny the facts, but by taking a breath, we get to decide how we are going to entertain them. Do what you can where you are with what you have and then hold the intention of what you would like to see happen. Listen to the part of you that will bring you good ideas.

One thing I know for sure is, everything happens for a reason. I have not always understood that, and sometimes I do not like it because I want to know why and what's going to come from it *now*. Have you ever felt that way? If you take a moment and think of the trials and the hard times you have gone through, you may find they were blessings, even if just for the learning and the growth you experienced. When having what you call a difficult experience, remind yourself that something good will come out of this.

Increase your faith by putting your panic on hold—a great teaching from my coach Mary that came from a life experience she was having. Mary and her husband had gone to a teaching. The presenter was speaking on how you could put your panic on hold. He said if you have something bad happening, do not panic. Put your panic on hold for three days. She thought it was crazy, and as she was sharing and teaching me this, I did too. She and her husband were panicking about a tough life situation that happened, and Mary remembered, "Wait, the teacher said we can hold our panic for three days." It was Tuesday at noon, so they scheduled their panic for Friday at noon. They then thought of what they could do and what would they love to see come out of this. By Thursday, not Friday, something greater emerged, and the issue was resolved. She finished with "I would have panicked, and I have learned that I don't have to." That story has been a game changer for myself and my clients. I don't do it perfectly, but I do it very well. I invite you to practice scheduling your panic. It will change your life and those around you.

CHAPTER 8

Fear vs. Faith

As I mentioned in the previous chapter on faith, I have learned in my studies that fear is also the opposite of faith. If we are feeling fearful and we stay there, we are not having faith. This doesn't mean we don't have our moments; we just want to be certain we don't stay there. We do that by being aware.

Fear is just letting us know that we are at the edge of what we have known. We experience fear when we are moving into the unknown, something new we haven't yet experienced in our lives. It's *okay* to feel some rattle or be uncomfortable. I repeat here that we want to be certain we don't stay there. Anybody that has what we consider "great success" has experienced that success by being willing to get uncomfortable. Most people are not willing to get uncomfortable to experience lives they would love. The magic is on the other side.

Think of a time you were feeling uneasy about doing something or experiencing something. You stepped through the fear and experienced great joy. I know many people, including myself, that have said and still say the following words, "I wished I would have done it sooner."

Like all of us, you have something you want to be, do, or have. Are you willing to step through the fear to experience it? A part of you might say no because what if they laugh at you? What if you fail? My invitation to you is for you to change that way of thinking. Speak to that part of you. What it if they said yes? What if it all worked out?

We have not been trained to ask empowering questions. We have been trained to think just the opposite. Have you ever noticed that we do this? As you go through your day, notice it. Don't judge it; just notice it. You will hear yourself or others say, "But what if it doesn't work? What if they say no? What if I get hurt?" Yes, we want to be smart in our decisions, but let yourself go to empowering questions. What if it did work?

What I learned when I am having a fear-based thought or moment is to *do it afraid*. Mary's son Matt taught me this when I was feeling fearful about doing things I had never done, which included speaking in front of people. What does that mean for you and my clients? What I do is get myself connected to the why—why am I doing it? I look at why I am doing it and come to the realization that my why and the end result that I am seeing for myself are far greater than the fear. So, *I do it afraid.* Remember, you can have fear without fear having you.

Another great thing I have learned and will serve you greatly is knowing you are not alone. The god, the source that is breathing you, wants you to experience the desires of your heart. As long as what you are working toward and what is calling to you is good and has good in it for you and others, you will get the support and have all that you will need. When you practice these ideas, they will become a part of you, and applying *faith* in your life will become normal to you.

CHAPTER 9

Intuition

I once heard it said that when we hold an intention for something that we would like to see come into our lives, that is what it means to pray. Intuition is the channel by which the higher power you are praying to answers you.

What I have learned for myself early on and for many people I have taught is, we don't sit quiet long enough to hear and receive the answers that we are seeking. The radio or the TV is on. We're on our electronic devices. We're busy doing chores, and we are just being busy at being busy. The Bible calls intuition the still, small voice. Gandhi called it the voice for truth, as long as we are willing to listen.

That is why I believe meditation is so important, not just speaking our prayers and using the practice of visualization, which is so important, but going quiet for even if just ten minutes to start.

Intuition is that inner knowing, that part of you that knows all—everything that ever was, is, and will be. Wouldn't it be a great idea to tap into that part of you? I like to call it my IGS (internal guidance system). We have a

GPS in our cars and on our phones, and we have one that is guiding us as well.

Some of my clients have shared with me that they don't have a good intuition. It doesn't speak to them, or they are not clear what voice is speaking to them. If we are of a sound, healthy mind, you have been gifted with this great mental faculty. The only question is, Do we know how to tap into that part of us and practice it long enough till we recognize its voice?

Pretend a friend calls you on the phone, and you haven't heard from them in a while. If they say hi to you without saying their name, you will know who it is right away. Why? You know that voice; you got familiar with that voice. You can do that with your intuitive voice (intuition).

We all have had times where we have said, "I just had a feeling" or "I could feel it in my gut." Some people say, "I have a sixth sense." We only have five senses. Intuition is not a sixth sense, but I can see where people think this way, for it does guide us if we let it.

I will share a funny story now, which might spark memories of our intuition at work. I was sitting in the living room watching a movie, and I could smell this amazing smell of baking. My wife Karen was making chocolate chip cookies, and her chocolate chip cookies are amazingly delicious. Karen invited me to have some. I jumped up like yes. I then poured myself a large glass of milk. My inner child coming out. :o) I placed my cookies and milk on my stand next to my lazy boy chair. My next thought was, *Let me wash up first.* As I got up, the voice said to me do not leave that there. I kept walking through the dining room, and on to the kitchen, the voice said again, "Do not leave that there." I ignored that voice twice nonetheless.

I came back from the washroom, and my milk was all over my cookies, my chair, and on the surge suppressor laying on the rug. I laughed out loud, for I knew better. You see, we had a cat named Mouse, and she was eighteen years old. She had never touched anything before, so no reason to think she would now. The thought never came to my mind. For some reason, this was the day. You see the intuitive voice was trying to tell me. Why? Because it knew without a doubt what was going to happen. I find it so empowering and liberating that we are connected to a power that does that for us. This part of us is connected to a source that knows all past, present, and future.

We all have many stories like this. When you are asked to take an umbrella, take a jacket, turn here, or turn there, and you hear that voice telling you not to do or say something, listen immediately. The more you do it, the more it will speak to you. That is what Gandhi meant when he said the voice for truth is as loud as our willingness to listen. Are you willing?

As you practice tuning in, listening and allowing that inner voice to guide you, I invite you take note of things I have learned. When trying to discern its voice remember this: Your intuition is loving, kind, caring, and life-giving. It is never boastful, loud, angry, or condemning. It just simply makes its statement with no judgment.

I can tell you without a doubt that my inner voice is guiding me now every day and all day. It talks to me constantly. I had a client say early on in her lessons that that would drive her nuts. We laughed as I explained that the voice is not like that. The voice is not interrupting; it just softly speaks to you and guides you. I cannot write you a guarantee, but I can promise you that if you truly take time to get to know this voice, life will get easier for you. Give yourself this gift. Start with ten minutes a day, and build up from there.

CHAPTER 10

Are You Deserving?

This is one of the hardest blocks that many of my clients including myself have faced. Not feeling deserving or good enough seems to run in the background, and this is a bit more subtle than some of the other challenges that we face.

The greatest words I heard about this was from my mentor Mary. She said that if you are breathing, then you are deserving. You do not have to do anything to be deserving; it is our birthright. When you first hear this, you may have a tendency to push back a little bit. That is okay and is something I have experienced often.

Think about it this way: Do you believe that what you call your higher power thinks that you are not deserving? Again, it doesn't matter what you call it. Can you, with your heart of hearts, say that the energy that breathes you, courses the blood through your veins, and brought you here believes you are not deserving? I can tell you the answer is an unequivocal *no*! I am asking you to trust me on this.

We pick up a sense of nondeserving along the way. We learn it from those around us, even from the people that are in positions to care for us. We learn it from TV, radio, and social media. Just because somebody is in what we call leadership positions or loved ones that let you take on that belief, it doesn't make it true—not for you anymore. Say these words repeatedly: I am deserving of a great life. If you are finding that you are not in a place of believing right now, then keep repeating it while you believe in my belief.

CHAPTER 11

The Law of Circulation/ Giving and Receiving

This chapter on the law of circulation is an important piece of our work here. Here, we will speak to giving and receiving. We want to have both channels open. All the greats have spoken to the importance of giving. In most religious environments, we are asked to tithe, which means giving 10 percent of the earnings we receive.

I can tell you I haven't heard very much about being a good receiver. As I was studying, I found I was not doing a very good job at either giving or receiving.

Along the way, I have met people in workshops and my courses who also were not doing very well. You may have the same thoughts they did: "I am not doing that" or "If I do that, I will not eat or I will struggle." I had one woman early on that proceeded to tell me that her mom and dad, her uncles, and other elders she knew have had a decent amount of success, and she never heard of this. She decided to take a deeper dive and ask questions and found out they were very giving. She then explained that it was not a church per se because they didn't belong to an organized religion or church of any kind.

I let her know as I am telling you here that it doesn't have to be a church, organization, non-profit, etc. You get to choose. Give to a place or person that will build on what you have given. She also thought that 10 percent was a stretch for her. I invited her to think about a percent she could start giving, even 1 percent. She replied, "I can do more than that." She chose 3 percent. I then asked her to record how much and where she was giving. It could be anything—a meal for a couple in a restaurant, giving to a foundation or a city mission that feeds people.

This call had taken place right before the Christmas holidays, and when she came back for her next session, she was so thrilled to share with me that she was already giving in so many areas. When she tracked and added it all up, she found it very easy to get to 10 percent.

I love how my mentor Mary puts it: When we are not giving, we create a kink in the hose that is stopping the flow of abundance that is trying to get to us. When we give, we are opening that door of abundance. When you are led to give or you get the impulse to do something special for someone, lean into it and take the action. I have found that I get more out of it than they do. Yes, giving opens the flow, but the feeling I get when I give is so rewarding.

The largest and most successful networking group in the world, BNI, has a vision statement. It is "Givers gain." If you give referrals to the members in your group, they in turn will want to give referrals to you.

Give, and it will be given to you: good measure, pressed down, shaken together, and running over will be put into your bosom. For with the same measure that you use, it will be measured back to you. (Luke 6:38, New King James Version)

Bring the whole tithe into the storehouse, that there may be food in my house. *Test me in this," says the Lord Almighty,* "and see if I will not throw open the floodgates of heaven and pour out so much blessing that there will not be room enough to store it. (Malachi 3:10, New International Version; emphasis mine)

Now, let's talk about how we can be a good receiver. As I stated earlier, I had never heard this. To be a good receiver, it starts with receiving what you are being given and saying thank you. Here are some examples: Someone buys you a gift, and it is not even your birthday. We might say, "You really shouldn't have." Why did you do this? A friend or coworker meets you for lunch, and they offer to treat you. They say to you, "I got this." We not only say no but we also fight for the check.

Someone pays you a compliment. I was in a large business meeting, and I was talking to a woman, and others were coming around. Several people complimented her on the blouse she was wearing. She turned to them and said, "Oh, this old thing" as she was waving them off.

Start finding ways to move into being a gracious receiver. This will up level your sense of deserving as well. In the book called *The 5 Love Languages*, giving is one of those languages. If this is a person's love language, we don't want to be preventing them from expressing this part of who they are.

I will end with saying I was the person that would fight for the check. I can tell you that I am a gracious receiver now, as well as being a systematic giver. The returns you will experience are tenfold.

CHAPTER 12

Forgiveness

It is no surprise that you will find forgiveness as a key component of all teachings covering personal growth—books, seminars, retreats, counseling, religious organizations, AA, you name it.

Why is forgiveness so important? The lack of forgiveness and carrying around resentment are two of our biggest blocks to us having a happy, fulfilling, successful life. I have had countless people in my programs with what we would call have horrible things happen to them, even from the people that were supposed to be their caretakers. If this is you, I am sorry that was part of your experience in life. They told me I will never ever, ever forgive them. Perhaps you have felt that way. I know I have. Maybe you feel that way now.

Have you heard the following sayings? "Unforgiveness is like holding a hot coal in your hands and expecting the other person to get burned." The other one is, "It's like drinking poison and expecting the other person to die." You may be thinking, *How cliché*. I totally get it, and I felt that way too.

You are reading this book because you want to experience the best life has to offer, right? This is part of it. It cannot be skipped or ignored. You do not have to call or reconnect to the person or institution that hurt you or did you wrong. They may not even be here in a physical presence anymore. You can do it in the silence of your own comfortable space.

I have had clients write a letter and then burn it in a bowl. When the resentment comes back, you can say, "No, I put that down when I burned it in the bowl." For other clients, I have invited them to put a chair across from their chair and have the conversation. Again, it is not easy, but it is critical to our growth and creating the lives we would *love*.

What we like to call a person that has hurt us in the past or even right now in the moment is, they are being unskillful. I know you have other names for them, and believe me I have heard them; and at times in my life, I have felt the same way. Some of the stories I have heard have moved me to tears as we would talk about the story, but the true goal was to set it down. Some have said to me, "I cannot carry this around anymore. Can you help me?" My answer is always yes, even if the unforgiveness you have is for yourself.

The truth is, all these people or organizations that hurt us were being unskillful, and even when we did things to others or ourselves, we were being unskillful. When a person is being unskillful, they are crying out. My mentor taught me that they were calling for love.

A person doesn't act unskillful unless they have something going on in them that is causing it. And most likely, they have learned it, and that is how they act now. You might be thinking that is no excuse for they know better. A big one for me is having a thought that yes, they should know better, or maybe you know that they know better because they had done it in the past and apologized. Even if this is true, they were or are not disciplined (skillful) enough to get themselves to do better. Learning this was another game changer for me.

Our work is to take care of ourselves while others are being unskillful. Remember, we react because we have not learned and trained ourselves to respond how we would want to. We do not have to get upset because somebody did or said something to us. We can stay in the frequency and the vibration we choose. That is what the masters do. Remember, we don't have to do it perfectly.

So how do we forgive somebody in the moment? Notice that they are being unskillful. We can move to a place of compassion because something must be wrong, either in that moment or in the person's life. Have you ever had a person be so rude or angry, and you are like, What is his or her problem? Somebody tells you or you hear later what had happened to the person. Did you find yourself moving to "Oh no that is such a shame"? Probably yes, because I know I have. Once I knew the story, I moved to compassion. What if we could move to compassion without having to know the story? My learning this and applying it to my daily life changed everything for me, and it has for my clients as well.

My greatest go-to practice when in the moment is Mother Teresa's "love them anyway." When I get cut off in traffic or someone is short with me, I take a breath and say, "Love them anyway." Sometimes, it would take many breaths. But I stay in the breathes with "*love them anyway*," until I get back to the vibration of loving them anyway. That's the vibration I want to be in.

Another great tool that I use regularly and teach my clients is from the late great Dr. Wayne Dyer. This is a great one when someone is telling you that someone said something bad about you. We find ourselves hurt because we cannot believe someone did this. Dr. Wayne Dyer said, "What others say or think about me is none of my business." You may be thinking, *Wow, that would be hard to do.* Like anything, it will take practice, but learning this alone will change your life.

Another great tool comes from a story I heard about Eleanor Roosevelt. She is revered to be one of the greatest first ladies in our history because of her contribution to our country. People and the media complained about her dressing habits and used words for her as being gangly and such. A reporter that took a liking to her asked Eleanor, "Why don't you do something? Why don't you change this? You're married to the most powerful man on earth." Eleanor's reply was another tool that has stayed with me. Pay no attention to them. "All the water in the world cannot drown you unless you let it get inside of you." You, too, can have this power if that is what you decide. Why not decide it now?

These tools have added to my having a happy life. You can apply them as well. Like anything, it takes practice.

People have climbed Mount Everest, and they did it one step at a time.

Client Stories

I had a client that shared with me that he was a road ragger. Like, a crazy road rager. If he were cut off, he would find a way to cut them off. If they were driving too slow, he would eventually get in front of them and then go slow. Crazy, right? No, unskillful.

If you met him, you wouldn't have guessed or believe this about him. He shared this and many other stories where he was being unskillful. We went to work on this right away, and in a noticeably short period of time, this knee-jerk reaction started to decrease. Within in a couple of months, he called to share with me that he doesn't do it at all anymore. He just gives thanks for being safe in the moment and carries on. He is now applying those same skills to all areas of his life. Not long after, I came across his wife at an event, and she gave me the most heartfelt thank-you. In a kidding but grateful way, she asked me, "What did you do to my husband?" :o)

My next story includes multiple clients—young, old, male, and females. "I don't want to host the family events or go to family holiday parties. My family or significant others family are jerks (unskillful) and always do or say something that angers me." (Note: another person cannot make you angry unless you let them.) What I have taught them was first, you don't have to go, but if you have decided to go, visualize a pleasant experience. Do not expect people to be unskillful, and do not prepare yourself to be upset and have a terrible experience as you have been doing. You are not only expecting it, but you are also attracting it by expecting it.

Remember, we attract what we are being, and we attract what we are sending out. We/you get to control the vibration and frequency you are in. This is our work. We are learning life mastery skills here. If we move to somebody's lower frequency and vibration, we have given them our power. Stay at your high vibration, and you will bring the frequency up in the room. Even if you're right, you don't have to fight for it; knowing you're right is good enough. You can then go talk with someone else or go into another room.

I had several clients over the years and some now that are turning this around. One client practiced what we are discussing here. She visualized a fun time going to a family gathering where the mother and sisters-in-law were jerks (unskillful). She decided to enjoy herself despite their unskillfulness. She called me to inform me that nothing happened. She could not believe it and said to me, *"I got the power."* I laughed saying, "Yes, you do, but that is not the take on this." So what happened here? Their subconscious picked up on the idea that she was going to be happy no matter what, so they never went there. That was what she meant by having the power. It has been two years since this event where she got the power, and everything has been great ever since.

Some of my clients have said, after making such changes and other people might even say at first bluff, she was the problem. Not true. When we stand in our frequency, our power, and we present a confidence and decide we will not be moved, others respond. The beauty is for the people that continued to have negative experiences, did not react, and were not moved, so those experiences and relationships changed as well. Have you ever heard the saying "Just ignore them"? It means don't let them affect you, and it will most likely stop.

Another story is about people that are in relationships with people that are miserable and unhappy (unskillful) and taking it out on significant others and children. I had numerous clients make these great changes, but it starts with us. Yes, even if we are not the problem. This doesn't mean we stay in an abusive relationship or an unsafe environment. One client had a wife that would just scream when something was not going to her liking or she wanted something from him or the kids. She literally would throw tantrums. They would react, fight back, defend themselves, and plead their case but to no avail. I explained to him that this was just a pattern she learned and that being that way may have worked for a time. Through this work, I pointed out to him that he and the kids were not the issue. She was being unskillful for a reason. When she was acting this way, she was calling for love but didn't know it. "Just move away and teach your kids to do the same." The client let me know after just a couple of weeks that she would be standing there screaming with no one around. One time he looked in from around the corner and seen his wife catching herself looking around, and then she went quiet. After those couple of weeks, things started to change. You see, she had to look at herself. They then started to have conversations on how they could do it differently. How they and the kids could support one another in a more skillful way. It has been over a year now, and they have been doing it differently. He said, "Coach, you would not believe the change in her and in our home." I replied, "I wouldn't." :o)

What I learned when studying what we call unskillful people and people that are skillful is that we all have our moments. Yes, some more than others. You might even say you know people that are always unskillful, miserable, etc. This is the time to move to compassion. Moving to compassion is the beginning of forgiveness (i.e., not sure what is going on with them, but my heart goes out to somebody living life that way.) *Love them anyway!*

Another great revelation that came to me through this study was the difference between a person being skillful and unskillful is that connection to source and universal presence. Notice the word here, *universe* (*uni*-verse), meaning "one verse." In the process of working with people, it became clear to me that people being unskillful on a regular, continual basis are not feeling connected to the source that breathes them. They also are not connected to a purpose, a vision, or a dream, and they feel separated from others. The people that are connected to what breathes them feel included. You will hear them say, "We are one." They have a purpose, a vision, and a dream, and they feel connected with others, and they are happier. One of my greatest joys is helping people understand this.

Being resentful and unforgiving has destroyed countless lives and still does. I want to point out to you that this does not mean that we let people walk all over us. We want to take care of ourselves by making the choices we need to be safe and in healthy environments. Whenever you are feeling unforgiving or resentful, please come back to this chapter.

CHAPTER 13

Stages of Awareness

Early on in my study, I heard someone say if you were not growing, you were dying. This meant if we were not taking deliberate action to move forward and grow in life, we would go backward. More importantly, we would not experience the great things that life has to offer.

There is a Buddha teaching that covers this ever so greatly. It is the four stages of awareness. Buddha's teachings are primarily about being awake. He didn't mean waking up from a night's sleep. He was referring to our minds. There was a story where people were asking Buddha if he was a god. He replied *no*. They went on to ask him if he was an angel. He replied no. Then with frustration, they asked then, "What are you, man?" He said, "I am *awake*." Being awake to me means being aware. Aware is the way I like to say it.

Let us now go over the four stages of awareness, as I have come to understand them. Keep in mind we all move in and out of these awareness stages at times throughout our day, but our goal here is to evolve and move into higher stages of awareness and stay in them more often. As we apply the stages and are learning them, we will notice when we are in a lower stage of awareness, which means we can change them.

Mary always said to us to be aware of what we're being aware of. Notice what you're noticing. Don't judge it; just notice it. The four stages of awareness are to me, by me, through me, and as me.

1. Why Me: In this stage of awareness, we are more in the mindset of being a victim. We are more in a not happy/sleepy state complaining, "This always happens to me" or "Why are they doing this to me?" "Poor, poor me" type feelings reside in this stage. In this stage we are in a victim role. This comprises of very low frequencies and vibrations, and unfortunately, we attract more of the things that match it.

2. By Me: In this stage, we start to take more responsibility for what we are experiencing and have experienced in our lives. I call this the fun stage. You realize you are a cocreator, and you can start calling in the life you would love. In this stage, you begin to ask and then see what you ask for showing up. In this stage, the evidence of the law of attraction begins to show up in your life.

3. Through Me: In this stage, we are feeling more like we are a part of the universe. We move into feelings of being one with source energy and all that is around us. We feel included and not separate from universal presence and others. We feel that life is

moving through us. Yes, we are still experiencing the receiving of things we have asked for, but we are now moving more into celebrating who we are becoming, and we find ourselves being more giving to others.

4. As Me: This is the stage of awareness that all the great sages and saints have achieved. The gurus and life masters walk in this stage. We not only realize life is happening through us but that life is us. Life is moving through me, with me, as me. You realize that the same life energy that moved through the greats is in you. The people that are in this stage are not moved by circumstances. And when they have a circumstance, the impact is not as hard and lasts for a short period of time, if at all.

As you work on these stages, you will move back and forth through them. I have had so many clients tell me that when they started working with me, they were at the why me victim stage. Within months, they found themselves moving to the next stage and rarely going back to the "why me" stage. How liberating that was. I know it was for me. When you apply what you have been learning here, you, too, will experience moving into the higher stages more frequently and staying there longer. When you get to the higher stages, you will not be moved off or away from them easily.

This is one of my most recent stories of choosing to stay in my frequency and in the stage of as me. My wife noticed something on my back and asked me to have it checked out by my primary care physician. I had my annual checkup the next week. My doctor also didn't like the looks of it and sent me to a dermatologist right away. My wife Karen and I went to see him. With his many years in the practice, he noticed multiple places on my skin that he believed was melanoma (skin cancer). He made a call right in front of us to set up a call with the surgeon he recommended. He stepped out of the office. Karen asked me if I was okay. I said yes. She then asked me if I knew what he was saying to me. I said yes again. Karen was asking me that because it didn't really move me. The news didn't resonate with me, and I just knew that I would be well. I remember a time shortly after that feeling emotional.

You would think at first, *Now he gets it.* That was not the reason for this power of emotion that came over me. The strong feeling of emotion was coming from my moving to the realization that not only did I study this work and teach it every day but I was also living it. Since that day, I have had multiple surgeries, removing skin from my body that was not to the doctors liking, including one on my forehead—one I admit was not to my liking. What was to my liking was that nothing ever came of it, and for that I was grateful. Again, you won't, and we don't do it perfectly; but overtime, you will get better and better at it every day and get to experience living life in this way.

CHAPTER 14

Decision

To date, there have been thousands of books and chapters in books covering the word *decision* and how to make decisions. I have chosen to keep it probably as short as you will ever read. The dictionary definition is "the act or need for making up one's mind." You decided to buy this book. I invite you to not just enjoy it but apply the principles you are learning.

One of our greatest teachers Bob Proctor that I have mentioned at the opening not only talks about making decisions quickly but being disciplined. Bob's definition of discipline is "when a man or a woman gives themselves a command and follows it."

I like to ask myself and others this question: Are you doing the thing? You see the people that brought their dreams to life were doing the thing. It took Thomas Edison ten thousand tries before lighting the incandescent lightbulb and having it stay lit. Yes, ten thousand tries. What are you doing? What are you desiring to bring into your life? It starts with a decision—"I am doing this thing."

Here is one last thing worth sharing on this topic. People have said, "I am not Edison, Ford, Gates, or whomever." They were not what you know them to be when they started. They also didn't have anything that you do not possess or have the wherewithal to attract. They didn't have overnight success as some people may think. If you talk to a person that has had great success in life, in any field, most of them will tell you that it took them ten, twenty, thirty years, and so on to become that overnight success.

CHAPTER 15

Creating Your Vision: The Life You Love

Now that we have covered how we want to think and covered some areas that could be blocking us or keeping us stuck, it is time to create your vision-driven life. Here, you will want to write out your dream life, the life you love living.

Here, we will be covering the four domains of life: health, relationships, career, and time and money freedom. Before we get into the domains, I want to invite you to take some deep breaths and bring yourself to a peaceful state. Bring a big smile to your face. Think of something funny that happened or someone that you love or something that you love to do that is fun. The universe loves fun, and if we are going to write out the life we would love living, let us have some fun doing it. Give yourself permission.

The question around building your vision is, What would you love? Do not get hung up on the how. Remember, we don't have to know how. We have to know what. If we know what and we hold that in our minds, we will be guided on what steps to take.

Take all current and past conditions out of the equation, things like "I don't know the right people," "I don't have an education," "I am too young," or "I am too old." I don't have the right look or have enough money. Take all these conditions and any others and just toss them away. I want you to imagine that you have just rubbed Aladdin's lamp, and he has granted you three wishes. The funny thing about that tale is it wasn't only three wishes. There was no limit to the wishes.

The dream you are building and creating is three years from now (i.e., today is September 5, 2021. We are holding that all of our dreams are realized by September 5, 2024). Most people see changes right away and are well on their way within a year. We do three years out to quiet the voice or paradigm that says, "How are you going to do that?"

As you begin to create your vision and fill out what you would love in the four domains, ask yourself these questions: If you could do, be, and have all you desire, what would that look like? Where do you want to live? Who do you hang out with? What work are you doing? Is there a hobby you want to do more of? Do you travel? What do you drive? What do you wear? Do you give to a charity? What do you do for fun? If you woke up tomorrow morning living your best life, what does it look and feel like?

Feeling is especially important. What we think and speak with feeling on a regular continuous basis becomes a physical reality. "As a man thinketh in is heart, so is he." Let's go ahead and design that life now and be as grateful now as you would be if you woke up today with that life being your reality.

Life's Domains

Health

What would you love to see in your health? Maybe you are very happy with this part of your life. Your vision could be. I am so happy and grateful now that I continue my health practices, and I feel great.

If you are not experiencing what you would love, what would bring that in for you? Would you want to be more toned? Release extra weight, add a physical routine, or expand it and cut back or get off medicines. (Be sure to talk with your doctor about these goals).

Example with actions steps added in: I am so happy and grateful now that I have released twenty pounds by walking thirty minutes every day, working out at my gym for thirty minutes three days a week. I am also making healthier food choices while having two fun meals per week. I am also loving that I now have an abundance of energy and am doing what I choose.

Relationships

Think of your current relationships. If you are loving your current relationships in all areas, great. Your statement here could be "I am so happy and grateful now that I am experiencing wonderfully abundant relationships. I continue to nourish and support my loved ones as we continue to grow and expand the love that we have for one another."

For those of you that would like to increase the love you have in your life with your partner, you want to be clear on what you would love here and be willing to do and be what you are asking.

Example: I am so happy and grateful that my partner and I are so loving of each other. We support each other's dreams; we have date nights and really enjoy each other's company. We love the outdoors. We are both on a continuous growth path and love our lives together.

For those of you that are saying "but I don't have a partner." You do; he or she is in your thoughts, and therefore, they exist. Be clear on the things you would like to be doing together. What are some things you like about how they are or how they look? Yes, it is okay for you to ask for what you find attractive in the physical. You want to create the image of that person and see and feel as if they are here in your presence. Remember, I called my wife in, and I have had many clients do the same.

One client comes to mind that started working with me five years ago. She was almost forty years young and really was doing great in all areas of her life—abundant health, great career, beautiful home, and the material things she wanted as well as all other relationships being wonderful—but she just wasn't having success bringing in her partner.

She said, "This is all I want to work on." We got truly clear on what she wanted. Much of our early building of what she wanted came out of what she didn't want. She knew clearly what she didn't want by her past experiences. Once we were clear, she read her statement day and night and prepared herself for her love partner coming in. She met him three weeks into our program, and they were married the next summer. Your past does not determine your future unless you let it. If you are desiring a partner, you can and will have one if you so decide.

More on relationships, if you would like to rekindle a relationship—be it with parents, brothers, sisters, and old friends—write this in your relationships, and it will lead you to action if you really want it.

I have had many clients change relationships in this way. One client hadn't spoken with her brother in twenty years. We concluded that what happened and whose fault it was no longer mattered. The goal and the dream was rekindling that relationship in whatever way she could. This took some action steps. If he wasn't doing anything, she would have to reach out. She did, and they cried on the phone. They have since joined families and now get-together regularly. Yes, it took courage. Yes, she swallowed some pride, but pride and lack of courage weren't getting her to her goal.

As you continue to write out your vision, action steps will all be within the vision. Take the action you know to take, and you will be shown the next step.

Career

What would you love with your career? For those of you loving your career, speak to that: "I am so happy and grateful I am doing what I love, and I am rewarded greatly. I earn five thousand dollars, ten thousand dollars, or a hundred thousand dollars (your goal) per month or more for the service I provide. I continue to grow and learn in my field, and for that, I am grateful."

For those of you desiring more ("Rob, I do not like my job. I want to earn more money for myself and my family. I want to do something I enjoy), maybe you want to start a business or do something new. Speak it here. If you do not know exactly what that is right now, you can ask for guidance. Take time to meditate on it daily. Ask God or the universe, "What would you have me do? I am open to new ideas, and I am going to take the action as it presents itself." Maybe you have had an idea to do something for a long time, but you didn't think you could, or fear stopped you.

Example: You always wanted to be a nurse like my client I mentioned in an earlier chapter, you can speak it here. "I am so happy and grateful I am now a nurse. I love what I do, I am rewarded greatly, and it brings me so much joy." You now want to take the steps that will get you there. One step at a time.

If you like your job and you are earning what you like but find yourself not liking something about it, find things you do like. Focus on those things, and you will feel much better. I have found when I focus on the things I like, the things I don't like fall away.

Time and Money Freedom

In this domain, I have found that many people have one or the other, but not both. Did you know that you can have money and the time to enjoy it? I have met millionaires that work every day all week and have created a habit of no downtime, including taking time out for the family.

One gentleman, just six months ago, came to me saying, "Please help me. I change this, or I lose my wife. We love each other, but she told me her and my two young children need me in their lives, and she doesn't feel I am with them enough." I have also met many people that have a lot of time but would like more money to do the things they love.

Example: I am so happy and grateful that I get to enjoy time with my family. We are obligation-free and have the finances to do the things we love to do. Many of my clients choose to phrase it this way, "I am so happy and grateful that I am financially free. My family and I enjoy having weekend camping getaways. We have gone to Disney World as well as other great parks. We have a cabin in the woods or a condo on or near the beach. We both have new comfortable cars to drive. Our home is wonderful, and we have a great big pool and hot tub in the yard. We also have been blessed in a way that we give to our favorite charity and are quick to help others. When we see a need we fill it, and we receive great joy filling that need."

This domain is about your thinking about what time and money freedom looks like to you. What would you *love*? Getting clear on what we love is what will help bring it in. The universe loves specificity. I provided examples for you here. These examples may not be what you are desiring, so just change the words.

As I mentioned when we started, remember to have fun with this. Create in your mind what you would love.

Write it down and read it daily, in the morning when you awaken and in the evening as you go to sleep. While reading your vision, visualize its arrival and feel the feeling as if you are living that life now. Be as grateful now while you are calling it in as if it were already here. Remember, being grateful opens the door for good things to come to us.

At the bottom of your vision statement, write the statement below. This allows the great universal energy to do its work. Would it be okay if you achieved everything in your vision in a different way, faster, or on a greater scale? Yes, great! Then put this at the bottom: *This or something even greater still!*

I want to close this chapter by congratulating you for writing out your vision. Do not take a pass on doing this. Napoleon Hill from *Think and Grow Rich* stated that if a person writes out their vision just one time, they increase the receiving of it by 50 percent. Imagine if you did this daily.

There are people wanting to do, be, and have more but are not willing to do what it takes to get there. The people that are living the lives they truly love are not lucky. They didn't get there by chance. Like myself, I changed the way I was thinking and the way I was looking at things, and the things I looked at changed. A thought came to me to write this book. The paradigm said, "Who are you to write a book?" I spoke back to that voice, letting it know that I was a part of this great power, and I am doing this thing. You have that same power in you.

CHAPTER 16

Having a Support System

Having a support system while you are applying these principles, I believe, is crucial. In the beginning of this book, I shared my story of being a great study of the Law of Attraction. Yes, I was doing a great job learning, but what brought me to the next level where it has become a part of me is having a support system.

That is why I hired Mary to be my coach. Mary and her team were instrumental in my getting to the next level. We have a saying that "coaches have coaches." Mary has a coach. Bob Proctor has a coach. Tony Robbins has a coach. Successful athletes and entertainers have coaches. I share this, for this book will get you on your way. It would be an honor serving you in this way. It doesn't have to be me. Find someone that will be this person for you as you are learning to make this part of your daily life.

Why is this important? The hundreds of people I have helped needed support while they were learning, breaking through their fears, and busting down paradigms and habitual patterns. Many clients didn't know what was blocking them. Many of my clients called me regularly, but over the years, they now tell me stories of how they handle life situations. They used the tools that I have shared with you in this book. Everybody that was experiencing great success in life will tell you they had a mentor or coach, that someone special that they could learn from. Do not let yourself off the hook on this. Find that special someone to be your mentor, your guide.

CHAPTER 17

My Daily Practice

In the following pages, I will share my simple seven-step process to incorporate the laws and principles I shared here with you throughout this book. Before I share these, I want you to take another look at the book title: *We Do Come with Directions: Instructions for a Happy Life*. I repeat here that the word *direction* is defined as "the path that something or someone takes, the path that must be taken to reach a specific place, the way in which something is starting to develop or the way you are facing." After reading this book and creating your vision, your mind has changed. You are now facing the way you want to go.

You can now apply the instructions given inside this book. *Instruction*, or *instructions*, is defined as "detailed information telling how something should be done, operated, or assembled." You now have the tools assembled in your brain. You can operate these tools to bring in the life you love. Don't judge yourself if you don't do it perfectly. Nobody does it perfectly. If you stay aware, you will get better and better every day.

While you are bringing in your vision-driven life and you start to experience the manifestation of the great life you are creating, remember to enjoy the journey.

My Daily Practice

As I continue to learn from our masters, past and present, I have set up a daily morning practice that has been life-giving. It keeps me in a solid state to apply the principles I have learned. I share this in my seminars, online videos, and with all my clients. Before you go on to read this, understand these practices do not take long. Once you know them and incorporate them into your daily life, your subconscious will do them automatically for you.

1. Forgiveness

I was raised in a Catholic home, and it was customary to recite the Lord's Prayer, "Our Father." It became such a part of me growing up that I wake up with it in the morning. Not a bad thing, but I chose to change it up. I call it Rob's clearing-the-field meditation. As I stated before, release resentment and any unforgiveness, and you will open up the channels for more good to come to you.

Here is my clearing-the-field meditation:

- I forgive all others for any trespasses toward me, including the ones I am not aware of.

- I ask for forgiveness from all people that I have hurt in any way. Please send them love and goodwill, including people I have hurt and am not aware I did.
- God, universe, infinite source, I ask that you forgive me for all my shortcomings, and I ask that you shed the light of awareness on the things that I can improve on. I also ask that you bring awareness to me when I am about to do or say something that doesn't match my vision of who I want to be in the world.
- (Input your name here), I love you, and I forgive you. I know you are always doing your best. I am proud of you and the work you are doing in the world.

The field has been cleared. I can move freely into my day as I bring my gifts to the world. I feel happy, I feel healthy, and I feel terrific. :o)

If you did this every day for thirty days, you would see a great shift in how you feel and you would most likely decide to continue with it. I still find it liberating.

2. Be grateful

Write down or say ten things you are grateful for every morning and evening. This will set your mind to a frequency of being grateful and finding things to be grateful for. Remember, the more grateful you are, the more you get to be grateful for.

3. Vision

Your dream—read your vision every day and night. Feel the feeling of being the man or woman living that life. If you woke up living that life, how would you feel? Bring yourself to that feeling.

4. Physical movement

Start where you can—thirty minutes of walking, beginner's yoga, biking, or working out at the gym.

5. Meditate

Fifteen to thirty minutes of quiet time. Quiet your mind. This will connect you to your source. Great power and knowledge will open up for you here. Give yourself this gift.

6. Study

You want to have a great life? Study, read, and listen to self-development and positive energy–information every day. In today's world, this is easy. Listen in the car. Read on the bus. Listen while folding laundry. Watch something on YouTube. Just starting with one page or a fifteen-minute podcast or Audible. You can build up from there. If you are like me, you will get hungry for more and add more time to your routine.

7. Be a person of increase

This I learned from this work, which included a great piece by Wallace D. Wattles called *The Science of Getting Rich*. I have read this book hundreds of times, and I invite you to do the same. It can be one of the pieces you study from step 6. Being a person of increase simply means to be a person of increase in everything that you do, in every interaction that you have with others. Be pleasant, compliment others, tip well, encourage others, and in a business transaction, give more than you are receiving. Help others where you can and find ways to give. My promise to you here is, you cannot be a person of increase and not receive increase. There is a law of circulation that makes this so.

Again, at first, your paradigm might be telling you that you do not have the time to do this. Remember, if you learn anything and do it regularly, it will become automatic. I cannot express how important a practice as simple as this can be. It will change your life for the better exponentially and will also benefit those around you. Even if you are having a good life, these practices will make it a great life.

Closing Remarks

Writing this book has brought me the greatest joy. The joy comes in sharing what I have learned thus far and seeing what I know it can do for you as you apply what I have shared here. I invite you to read this over and over and go back frequently to the parts that resonated with you the most. Remember that voice that said to me, "Who are you to write a book?" That voice, paradigm, and limiting belief is now silent. :o)

There are millions of people in the world that are looking to improve their lives in one or all of the four life domains listed in chapter 15, "Creating Your Vision." They are looking for a sign or something magical to happen. The reason is that it could never be as easy as people are saying it is or as easy as starting to apply what you have learned here. They would be right in that it takes a decision, and it takes discipline to study and apply what you have learned here. If it were easy, everyone would be doing it. I can tell you this: it is not difficult, and it will get easier and easier as you do it daily. Now that I know what I do know, I think living a life by default, not by design, is much, much harder. I cannot write you a guarantee, but I can promise you this: *this works if you work it.* Anything that you do now and do well, there was a time in your life that you had never done it before—walking, talking, reading, riding a bike, driving a car, and many other things.

People that are having happy, successful lives are doing the things that make it so. They have a purpose and a vision for the lives they would love living. They are grateful and feel that they are one with everyone else and the universe. They see silver linings in tough times. Faith tells them they are not alone and that it will all work out. Happy people are loving and giving. They have learned not to hold resentments and move to forgiveness very quickly, and they make it a practice to love unskillful people anyway. Successful people *do it afraid* in service of their dream, and they take action even when they are uncomfortable. Successful people have mentors/coaches and apply the life lessons they are taught. Remember, we do not do this perfectly. Just continue to do better today than you did yesterday.

I have mentioned I have worked with the greatest people in this industry and have seen thousands of lives transformed. In my life coaching business, I have had the privilege, the pleasure, and the greatest joy of helping hundreds of people.

I will leave you now with this: If even a part of you is thinking, *I am not sure I can do this, learn this, and apply this way of thinking into my life*, know that as long as you have the desire to do so, you will. Henry Ford said, "Whether you think you can or you think you can't, you are right."

If ever you should have a feeling of not believing, please come back to these words: *believe in my belief.*

The end for now and your new beginning!

About the Author

Rob Ciminelli currently resides in Western New York with his wife, Karen. He enjoys spending time with his family, especially his grandchildren. He loves to travel. When he is not traveling, he enjoys spending time in nature out at his lake camp.

Rob is an award-winning certified life coach, and he finds it extremely rewarding to assist people in living their best life. Rob has had the distinct pleasure of learning from some of the greatest self-development teachers in this industry. You can find out more about Rob at www.resultswithrob.com.

www.ingramcontent.com/pod-product-compliance
Lightning Source LLC
Chambersburg PA
CBHW021114130726
47988CB00003B/1014